FOOD IN FOCUS

Milk and Yoghurt

Hazel King

First published in Great Britain by Heinemann Library
Halley Court, Jordan Hill, Oxford OX2 8EJ,
a division of Reed Educational and Professional Publishing Ltd.

Heinemann is a registered trademark of Reed Educational and
Professional Publishing Ltd.

OXFORD FLORENCE PRAGUE MADRID ATHENS
MELBOURNE AUCKLAND KUALA LUMPUR SINGAPORE TOKYO
IBADAN NAIROBI KAMPALA JOHANNESBURG GABORONE
PORTSMOUTH NH (USA) CHICAGO MEXICO CITY SAO PAULO

Designed by Celia Floyd
Illustrations by Sue Aldridge, Oxford Illustrators, p. 8 and Barry Atkinson, pp. 11, 13,
20, 21, 22, 23, 26, 28
Printed in Hong Kong / China

02 01 00 99 98
10 9 8 7 6 5 4 3 2 1

ISBN 0 431 08876 4

British Library Cataloguing in Publication Data

King, Hazel
    Milk and yoghurt. - (Food in focus)
    1.Milk - Juvenile literature   2. Yoghurt –
    Juvenile literature
    I.Title
    637.1

Acknowledgements

The Publishers would like to thank the following for permission to reproduce
photographs:

Gareth Boden, pp. 4, 7, 16, 18, 19, 25, 27, 28; Trevor Clifford, p. 5; Robert Harding
Picture Library, p. 21; Hulton-Deutsch, p. 6; National Dairy Council, p. 15; Tony Stone,
pp. 10, 12 (Graeme Norways); Trip, p. 9 (H. Rogers); Zefa, p. 13.

Cover photograph: Trevor Clifford

Every effort has been made to contact copyright holders of any material reproduced in
this book. Any omissions will be rectified in subsequent printings if notice is given to
the Publisher.

Contents

• •

Some words are shown in bold, **like this**. You can find out what they mean by looking in the Glossary.

Introduction

● ●

Milk is really quite amazing! It is the only form of nourishment a newborn baby needs, because human milk contains the correct balance of **nutrients** for a baby to survive the first weeks of life.

Most of us carry on having milk in our diet because we can use the milk of other mammals. Mammals are animals that feed their young with their own milk – just like humans. Some of the mammals that produce milk are cows, sheep, goats, buffalo, reindeer, camels, llamas and horses. Each animal produces milk that is exactly suited to the needs of its young.

A great deal of cows' milk is used today, as a drink, in cooking or for other products such as butter, yoghurt, cheese and cream.

Some people find they are **allergic** to animals' milk so they might use **soya milk** instead, produced from the soya bean. Because it comes from a plant, some vegetarians prefer to use this too.

Milk from goats, ewes and water buffalo is also used for drinking or making cheese.

Different types of milk and milk products

Milk is a very versatile product because it can be used in lots of different ways. As a drink, milk can be used for milkshakes, hot chocolate or frothy cappuccino coffee. Both sweet and savoury dishes can be made with milk which is why it is so useful. Sweet foods include egg custard, crème caramel, rice pudding and fudge. Even some biscuits have milk added to them. Savoury foods made with milk include lasagne, quiche lorraine, fish pie, bread rolls and some soups. Milk can also be used to make dishes that can be served as either dinner or dessert! Some examples are soufflés, omelettes and pancakes.

For many years milk has been used to make other products. Cream, butter, cheese and yoghurt are all made from milk and are often called **dairy products**. These foods differ depending on the type of milk used to make them. For instance, you can get ewes' milk yoghurt and goats' milk cheese. Like milk, yoghurt can be used in a variety of different ways and in both sweet and savoury dishes.

A selection of products made from milk and yoghurt

In the past

People have used milk from animals since the beginning of history. However, as milk turns **sour** very easily, in the past it was impossible to keep it fresh. Milk turns sour because the **bacteria** it contains multiply very quickly and cause it to go bad, particularly if it is kept warm.

Some cattle diseases such as tuberculosis (TB) and brucellosis were passed to humans who drank milk that had turned sour. This caused the deaths of many people. Then, during the 1850s and 1860s, a French scientist called Louis Pasteur found that bacteria could be killed if the milk was heated. First he experimented with the bacteria in wine and then he moved on to milk. He discovered that if milk was heated all the disease-producing bacteria were destroyed.

The process developed by Louis Pasteur became known as '**pasteurization**' and it is still used now to make sure our milk is safe to drink. Today milk is pasteurized by heating it to 72°C for 15 seconds and then, to keep it fresh, it is cooled quickly to below 10°C.

Louis Pasteur working in his laboratory

Although the milk we buy has been pasteurized it must still be stored properly to keep it fresh. Milk and other **dairy products** should be stored in a refrigerator at a temperature of about 5°C. At this temperature bacteria multiply very slowly so milk can stay fresh for two or three days if stored properly.

Milk does not have a strong flavour of its own. It should be kept covered in the refrigerator because it can pick up the smell and flavour of other foods.

Bacteria

Bacteria are microscopic creatures, so small that thousands of them could fit on a pinhead. Bacteria are all around you, all the time. Some are quite harmless but others are harmful if they are allowed to multiply inside you or if you eat the poisons they produce. In a warm room one bacterium can grow into several million within just 24 hours!

Some bacteria are useful. You will discover later that harmless bacteria are actually needed to make yoghurt. Another dairy product that is made using bacteria is cheese.

Milk and cheese should be covered and stored in a refrigerator

Around the world

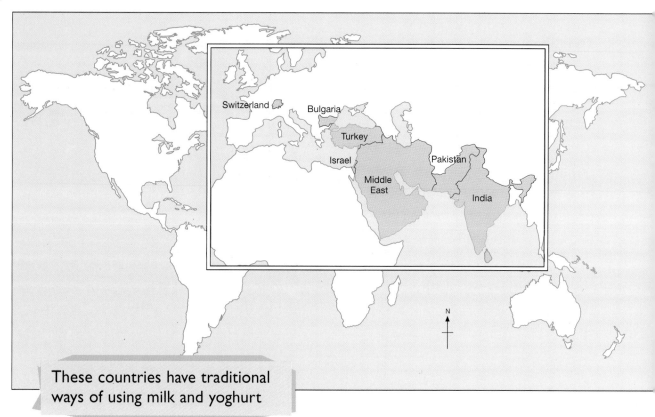

These countries have traditional ways of using milk and yoghurt

Both milk and yoghurt are widely used throughout the world although the type may vary (cows', sheep's, goats' etc). Like all food products, they tend to be used in different ways in different places, depending upon the culture and traditions of the country. However, because people travel and move about so much today, we are quite likely to use milk or yoghurt in a way that is not traditional for our country.

Bulgaria

Yoghurt is eaten a great deal here, which may be why Bulgarians are so healthy! It is used with salads, sauces and desserts. Bulgaria is said to produce the very best yoghurt.

Switzerland

The breakfast cereal, muesli, was invented in Switzerland. It is served with milk or yoghurt.

Turkey

A drink called *ayran*, made from yoghurt and iced water, is popular here.

Israel

Many Jewish people live according to strict religious laws which include what kind of food they are allowed to eat. Food which they can eat is called 'kosher'. One of these laws says that milk and meat must not be cooked or eaten together. Jews who strictly keep the laws have two sets of cooking utensils and wait three hours after eating a meal containing meat before eating anything containing milk or **dairy products**.

Pakistan

It is traditional to use yoghurt in meat dishes in Pakistan and India. The meat is put in a **marinade** of yoghurt and spices to make it tender.

India

Lassi is a refreshing yoghurt drink which often accompanies Indian meals. *Raita* is made from yoghurt, cucumber and mint and helps to cool spicy curries. At weddings many special foods are served, including *shrikhand*, a spiced yoghurt.

The Middle East

In this part of the world people regularly make yoghurt at home, from cows' or sheep's milk. They believe that eating yoghurt leads to a long and healthy life. A traditional Middle Eastern dish of stewed lamb is always served with yoghurt.

Yoghurt is used in lots of dishes from India

Making milk from grass

Dairy cows are female cattle that are kept for the purpose of producing milk. They are only able to give milk once they have given birth to a calf.

A great deal of the cows' day is spent chewing grass but they don't just do that for fun – they need grass to produce milk. Cows actually have four stomachs which are used to break down and digest grass. First the cow uses its tongue to tear off the grass and mix it with saliva. Once the grass is swallowed it is stored in the first two stomachs – the reticulum and the rumen.

The grass hasn't yet been chewed so the cow will **regurgitate** the grass (known as cud) in small mouthfuls and chew and swallow it again. This is known as 'chewing the cud'.

In the rumen the grass is broken down by digestive juices. The water is then removed in the next stomach, the omasum, and what is left passes to stomach number four, the abomasum.

Cows spend much of their time grazing on grass

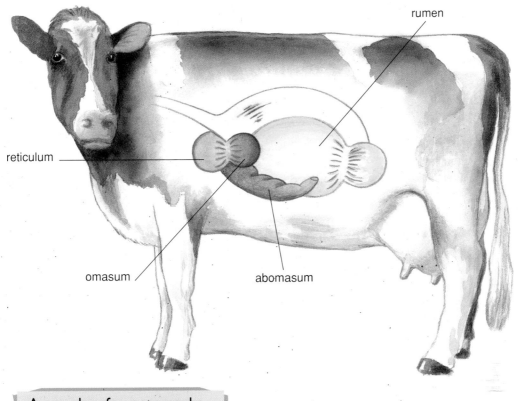

rumen

reticulum

omasum

abomasum

A cow has four stomachs

More digestion takes place until the **nutrients** from the grass are absorbed into the cow's bloodstream where they can be used to keep the cow healthy and to produce milk.

The milk gradually builds up, drop by drop, in the cow's udder until it is full and the cow is ready to be milked. On average each cow provides 4500 litres of milk every year.

Allergic to cow's milk?

Humans are the only creatures that feed their young on another creature's milk. Babies are often fed on a special powdered milk that is made from cows' milk but has been altered to suit human babies.

However, some people discover they are **allergic** to cows' milk and it may cause a reaction such as eczema, asthma, diarrhoea, arthritis, migraine or catarrh.

Other people avoid cows' milk because they are 'lactose intolerant'. Lactose is a type of sugar found in milk. It cannot be digested by everybody.

Instead of cows' milk, those with an allergy can have **soya milk**, goats' milk or sheep's milk and health food shops sell 'dairy-free' products including margarine, bread and cakes.

From cow to kitchen

• •

Once a cow has chewed all that grass and made lots of milk how does this become the milk you drink in your kitchen?

1 Cows are kept by farmers who supply milk to dairies, or to creameries for the manufacture of **dairy products**.

2 The cows have to be kept as clean as possible. They are milked twice a day, usually by machine, and the amount of milk each cow produces is recorded.

3 Milk from the cow passes to a refrigerated farm vat where it is cooled and stored. An insulated road tanker collects it the same day or the following morning.

Cows being milked by machine

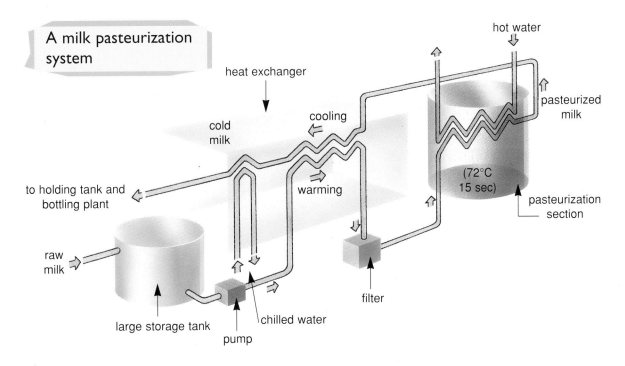

A milk pasteurization system

heat exchanger

hot water

cold milk

cooling

warming

pasteurized milk

to holding tank and bottling plant

(72°C 15 sec)

pasteurization section

raw milk

large storage tank

pump

chilled water

filter

4 On arrival at a dairy, the milk is tested to make sure it is clean and free from disease. If it passes the test the milk is unloaded into large storage tanks.

5 Next the milk is heat-treated using the **pasteurization** process which destroys harmful **bacteria** but hardly affects the **nutritional value** or taste of the milk.

6 The milk may then be processed further before being hygienically bottled or packed into cartons or containers.

7 The milk is packed in refrigerated lorries and taken to supermarkets, shops and other retailers.

8 **Consumers** can buy milk in all sorts of outlets from petrol stations to supermarkets, or they may have it delivered to their homes.

Containers are filled with milk and the tops are sealed

Making yoghurt

Yoghurt can be described as 'thickened milk' which has a sharp, tangy taste. Today it has a creamy, smooth texture which is very different from the yoghurt produced in the past. This was more like milk with lumps in it.

Just like milk, yoghurt is very versatile. It can be used for salads, sauces, desserts, breakfasts, in baking, as an **accompaniment** to a meal, even as a drink.

As yoghurt has a rather 'healthy' image, food manufacturers have developed a huge range of different types and flavours. Unfortunately these are not always as 'healthy' as they might seem because sugar and sugary foods are added to them, especially the children's varieties.

Yoghurt manufacture

1 Yoghurt is produced from whole milk or skimmed milk, depending on the type of yoghurt to be made.

2 The yoghurt is produced by adding a special **bacterial** culture, sometimes known as a 'starter culture', to the milk. These bacteria are harmless. Their proper name is *Lactobacillus bulgaricus*, taken from the country – Bulgaria – where yoghurt was first eaten.

3 The milk is heated to 43°C. At this temperature the bacteria cause the milk to set or 'clot' so that it looks a bit like thick custard. It then has to **incubate** for several hours.

4 After this, the yoghurt must be cooled very quickly to 5°C to stop any bacteria multiplying. It is stored at this temperature while it becomes slightly acid.

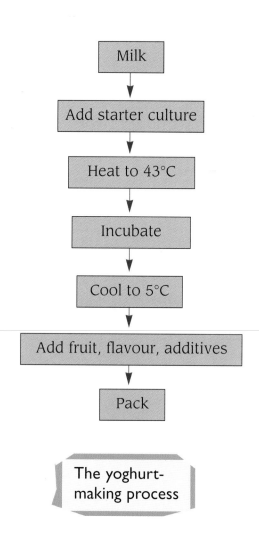

The yoghurt-making process

5 Additives may be added such as a colouring, thickening or **preservative** – check the ingredients list! Other ingredients that may be added include sugar, fruit purée or pieces, cereals and nuts.

6 The yoghurt is then poured into its pot and the lid is sealed down. It must be stored at a temperature of 4.5°C.

Sometimes the lid of a pack of yoghurt may bulge and the yoghurt inside may taste fizzy or gassy. This happens with time as the fruit starts to **ferment** and produce the gas carbon dioxide (CO_2). You should always eat yoghurts before the use-by date.

Yoghurt being produced in a factory

The finished product is packed up ready to go to the shops

What type of milk?

Today we can choose from a variety of milks. Each one has a useful purpose or is suited to a particular type of person. For example, skimmed milk is available for people on low-fat diets and thick, sweet, condensed milk is excellent for making confectionery, such as fudge.

Some of the different types of milk available

Whole milk

This is **pasteurized** milk that contains about 3.9% fat. Look carefully at a bottle of whole milk and you will see the fat or cream has floated to the top. This is because fat is lighter than milk.

Semi-skimmed milk

This is pasteurized milk with about half its fat removed so it only contains 1.5–1.8% fat. This means it is lower in **kilocalories** (**kilojoules**).

Skimmed milk

Again, this is pasteurized milk but with virtually all its fat removed, leaving just 0.1% fat. As it is low in calories it is ideal for someone wanting to lose weight; however, it is unsuitable for babies and young children.

Homogenized milk

To produce this type of milk, pasteurized whole milk undergoes a special process. The milk is forced through tiny holes to break up the fat. When it is left to stand, the fat does not rise to the top but remains floating throughout the milk.

Sterilized milk

In this process, milk is heated to 113°C and then homogenized. This gives it a slightly different flavour from non-sterilized milk. If unopened it will keep for several months.

Ultra heat-treated milk (UHT)

UHT milk is a type of **sterilized** milk. It is heated to 132.2°C for one second, then it is packed into special cartons. Like sterilized milk, if unopened it will keep for several months.

Evaporated milk

This is sterilized milk that has been concentrated or made thicker by **evaporation** (which removes some water). It is sold in cans and if unopened it will keep for many months.

Condensed milk

This is also concentrated milk but with sugar added to it, which helps to **preserve** it. Whole, semi-skimmed or skimmed milk is used. It is very thick and sweet.

Dried milk powder

Dried milk powder is a very useful store cupboard 'stand-by'. It is made from whole or skimmed milk which is homogenized, heat-treated and dried to remove all the water. When milk is needed, the dried powder is mixed with water to produce liquid milk.

Flavoured milk

Different types of flavoured milks are made from long-life (UHT or sterilized) or fresh milk which has flavourings added such as chocolate, strawberry or banana.

What type of yoghurt?

Yoghurt is very popular with both adults and children. This is probably because food manufacturers have come up with so many different varieties. You can buy yoghurt in all sorts of flavours; the pots come in all shapes and sizes and you can also stir in your own flavouring.

There are thick and creamy yoghurts, low fat yoghurts, set yoghurts, even some especially for breakfast. Here are just some of the yoghurts available.

Low fat, very low fat, diet or light yoghurts

These are made using skimmed milk and may be natural or flavoured. Flavoured yoghurts may have sugar added so they might not be as healthy as they sound.

Bio yoghurts

By adding extra cultures, a mild-tasting yoghurt is produced. These are thought to be particularly healthy as they are supposed to assist the digestion.

Set or French yoghurts

These yoghurts are heat-treated and sealed in the pot, where they are left to **ferment** and set. They have a more solid texture than other yoghurts.

Just a few varieties of yoghurt

Thick and creamy yoghurts

Whole milk is used to make these yoghurts, and some of them have cream added as well. They may be natural or flavoured.

Greek or Greek-style yoghurts

For a very rich flavour choose a Greek yoghurt! These are made with whole milk and have a high fat content.

Children's and infants' yoghurts

To attract children these yoghurts are usually sold in cartons covered with cartoon characters. They are usually made using a smooth purée of fruit rather than pieces and the infants' yoghurt should have a low sugar content. Children's yoghurt is available with (unhealthy!) sugary foods in the lid which can be stirred in.

Do-it-yourself yoghurt! Add the flavour to suit your taste

Split or corner yoghurt

Just to make eating more fun, you can now buy a pot of yoghurt with a separate corner containing a flavouring. You can add this to the yoghurt as and when you please! The flavouring might be fruit purée, cereal grains or chocolate-coated cereal.

Fromage frais

Although these can usually be found with the yoghurts and other cold desserts, in fact they are a form of soft cheese. Eaten as a pudding, they come in small pots containing a very creamy product that may be plain or lightly-flavoured. They were first eaten in France.

But is it good for you?

People often say milk is 'good for you' and what they are referring to is its **nutritional value**. The nutritional value of a food depends on the type and amount of **nutrients** it contains. Nutrients are the substances that are contained in food and are used by our bodies to stay alive and healthy.

Nutrients

The nutrients found in milk

protein
energy
vitamin B₁ (thiamin)
vitamin B₂ (riboflavin)
phosphorus

vitamin A
vitamin D
vitamin B₁₂
fat
calcium

Yoghurt contains the same nutrients because it is made from milk but the amounts will vary. Different types of milk and yoghurt will also contain different amounts of each nutrient.

Why are these nutrients important?

Energy	All food provides energy which is measured in **kilocalories** or **kilojoules**. Our body burns this energy all the time to keep us functioning properly.
Protein	This is needed for the formation, growth and repair of our body tissues.
Fat	Fat supplies us with lots of energy and helps our body to absorb vitamins. It also protects our **internal organs**.
Calcium and phosphorus	These are both minerals which work together to keep our bones and teeth strong.
Vitamin A	This vitamin is important for our eyes as well as for growth and a healthy skin.
Vitamin D	This vitamin is only found in small quantities in milk although you can buy varieties with 'added vitamin D'. It is required for our growth and development and for the formation of bones and teeth.
Vitamin B₁ Vitamin B₂	Both are needed to help the body release the energy that food supplies.
Vitamin B₁₂	This is essential for our growth and the formation of red blood cells and for our nervous system.

This girl is enjoying a glass of milk

Milk and yoghurt are found in the 'Eat moderately' section of the 'healthy diet pyramid'. This is because they contain protein and some fat as well as vitamins and minerals. We should try to eat a moderate amount every day. For example, a twelve-year-old boy might have milk on his cereal, a milkshake at lunchtime and a glass of milk with his evening meal.

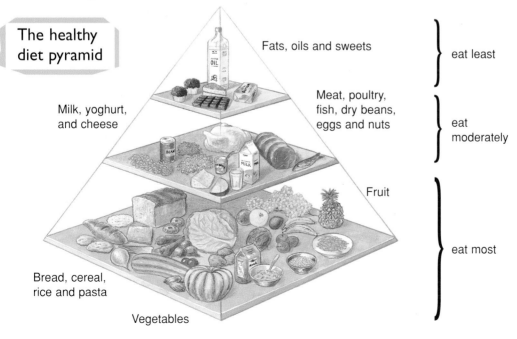

The healthy diet pyramid

Fats, oils and sweets — eat least

Meat, poultry, fish, dry beans, eggs and nuts — eat moderately

Milk, yoghurt, and cheese

Fruit

Bread, cereal, rice and pasta

Vegetables

eat most

Experimenting with milk

Using milk to make sauces or drinks often involves heating it in a saucepan. When milk is heated several changes occur. This experiment will help you to understand these changes. You must be very careful when using the cooker or hob. Tell an adult before you start.

Heating milk

Read through the experiment before you begin so that you know what to do.

Watch what happens very carefully!

You will need:

- about 300 ml milk
- 1 heavy-bottomed saucepan
- a cooker or hob
- 1 small bowl

What to do:

1 Pour the milk into the saucepan.
2 Heat the milk gently and watch very carefully. You should be looking out for:

- steam rising from the top of the milk
- a skin forming which may look wrinkled
- tiny bubbles around the edges of the saucepan and underneath the skin
- the milk rising up the sides of the saucepan.

3 Take the saucepan off the heat *before the milk boils over*.
4 Let the milk cool for a few minutes then pour it into the bowl.

What happened?

There are good reasons why all those changes took place. They could only happen because milk contains protein, fat, calcium and water.

When milk gets hot some of the water in it turns to steam. This is what you could see rising from the top of the milk. Because fat is lighter than milk, any fat will float to the surface. Did you notice it become a creamy colour?

Then the protein changes. Like all proteins, it 'sets' when it is heated and this is what makes the skin on the milk.

Now the milk has a 'lid' on it. As it boils the bubbles of steam underneath push the skin and force it upwards, making the milk look like it is growing.

This is what makes milk boil over so easily.

After pouring out the milk did you notice a layer on the bottom of the saucepan? Heating causes some of the protein and calcium in the milk to fall to the bottom where it settles. This will burn if you do not use a heavy-bottomed saucepan.

Watch out! Milk boils over easily

Milky shakes

Ice-cold milkshakes are nutritious and delicious, especially when you make them for yourself. They are popular with children and are drunk in countries in the western world.

You do not have to use a liquidizer to make these shakes but if you do, ask an adult to help you. You can serve milkshakes in tall glasses and you may choose to add decoration to make them look special. Each recipe serves two people.

Banana shake

Serves 2

You will need:

Ingredients

- 150 g pot natural yoghurt
- 2 medium bananas
- 300 ml fresh milk, chilled
- sprinkling of nutmeg for decoration

Equipment

- liquidizer (or hand whisk and a large bowl)
- 2 tall glasses

What to do:

1 Place the yoghurt, bananas and milk in the liquidizer and close the lid firmly. Blend for 30 seconds. (Or hand whisk the ingredients together in bowl.)
2 Pour into two glasses and sprinkle lightly with nutmeg.

Chocolate shake

Serves 2

You will need:

Ingredients

- 1 heaped teaspoon drinking chocolate
- $1\frac{1}{2}$ tablespoons boiling water
- 450 ml fresh milk, chilled
- 2 heaped tablespoons vanilla ice-cream

Equipment

- bowl
- teaspoon
- tablespoon
- balloon whisk
- 2 tall glasses

What to do:

1 Place the drinking chocolate in the bowl with the water and mix to a smooth paste with the teaspoon.
2 Pour in the milk and whisk together using the balloon whisk.
3 Add 1 tablespoon of vanilla ice-cream and whisk again.
4 Place the remaining ice-cream in the bottom of the glasses. Pour the milkshake over the ice-cream.
5 Serve immediately.

Sunshine shake

Serves 2

You will need:

Ingredients

- 300 ml fresh milk, chilled
- 150 ml pineapple juice, chilled
- 150 ml orange juice, chilled
- 1 teaspoon honey
- 2 slices of orange and sprigs of mint for decoration

Equipment

- liquidizer (or hand whisk and a large bowl)
- 2 tall glasses

What to do:

1 Whisk all the ingredients together.
2 Pour into the glasses and decorate with slices of orange and sprigs of mint.

Strawberry shake

Serves 2

You will need:

Ingredients

- 150 g pot strawberry yoghurt
- 300 ml fresh milk, chilled
- strawberry for decoration

Equipment

- liquidizer (or hand whisk and a large bowl)
- 2 tall glasses

What to do:

1 Whisk all the ingredients together.
2 Pour into the glasses and decorate with sliced strawberries.

Ice cold, home-made milkshakes

Hot baked sandwiches

Sandwiches are a well-known snack invented by the British Earl of Sandwich. The original idea has been changed and developed many times over the years. Why not try this version – sandwiches hot from the oven! Ask an adult to help you.

Just like ordinary sandwiches, there are lots of different fillings that can be used. For instance, if you do not like cheese and tomato you could use chopped bacon and sliced mushrooms or, if you do not like pickle, use tomato ketchup, brown sauce, mustard – whatever you fancy!

Cheesy sandwiches

Serves 1

You will need:

Ingredients

- 25 g cheese, e.g. Edam
- $\frac{1}{2}$ tomato
- 2 slices bread
- teaspoon of pickle (optional)
- a little butter or margarine
- 150 ml milk
- 1 egg
- black pepper (optional)

Equipment

- chopping board
- sharp knife
- spreading knife
- shallow ovenproof dish, approximately 15 cm x 10 cm
- measuring jug
- fork
- oven gloves
- spatula
- serving plate

What to do:

1 Check the shelf is in the middle of the oven. Set the oven at Gas Mark 4, 180°C.

2 Place the cheese on the chopping board and cut into slices. Slice the tomato.

3 Place the bread on the board and lay the cheese on one slice. Top with tomato slices. Spread the other slice of bread with pickle or chutney, if liked.

4 Place the bread with pickle on top of other piece, to make a sandwich. Lightly spread some margarine or butter over the top of the sandwich then carefully cut it into four triangles.

5 Rub a little butter or margarine around the bottom and sides of the dish then place the sandwich triangles in it. Measure the milk into the measuring jug. Break the egg into the milk and add a sprinkling of pepper, if liked. Whisk thoroughly using a fork. Pour this mixture all over the sandwich in the dish.

6 Using oven gloves, carefully place the dish in the oven on the middle shelf. Bake for 25 minutes. At the end of the cooking time the sandwich should be lightly browned and the egg mixture will have set.

7 Carefully remove the dish from the oven, using oven gloves. Place on a heatproof surface and allow to cool for one minute. Run a knife around the edges then carefully lift the sandwiches out with a spatula. Put on a plate and serve.

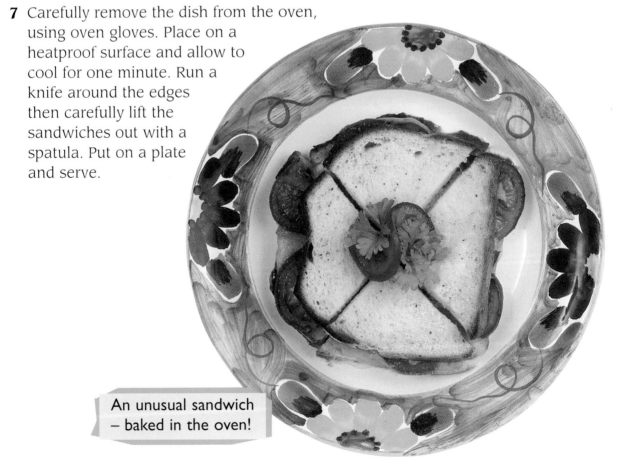

An unusual sandwich – baked in the oven!

Tilted jellies

These desserts look really interesting because the jelly layer is tilted at an angle.

Traditionally jelly is popular in America, Australia and Britain and is especially popular with children! Dessert jellies are usually fruit-flavoured and when they are ready for eating they have a special wobbly feel.

These jellies taste as good as they look!

Tilted jellies

Serves 4

You will need:

Ingredients

- water
- 1 x 135 g packet of your favourite flavour jelly
- fresh fruit such as a large banana, pear or peach, or about 150 g raspberries, strawberries, blackcurrants
- 4 level tablespoons custard powder
- 1 tablespoon caster sugar
- 600 ml semi-skimmed milk
- 4 tablespoons natural yoghurt
- chocolate buttons for decoration

Equipment

- kettle
- measuring jug
- knife
- chopping board
- 4 x 300 ml glasses or tall sundae dishes
- tablespoon
- small bowl
- saucepan
- teaspoon
- wooden spoon

What to do:

1 Fill the kettle and leave it to boil. Place the jelly in the measuring jug. Carefully pour on boiling water up to the 300 ml mark.

2 Stir until the jelly is dissolved. Top up to 600 ml with cold water. Stir again.

3 If necessary, wash the fruit and remove the stalks or peel. Chop into small pieces then divide among the four glasses.

4 Pour 150 ml of jelly over the fruit in each glass. Carefully prop the glasses in the refrigerator at an angle so the jelly can set tilted in the glass. Leave to set.

5 Meanwhile, make the custard by placing the custard powder in the small bowl with the caster sugar. Add some of the 600 ml of milk. Mix the custard powder and milk with a teaspoon until smooth. Pour the rest of the milk into the saucepan and heat gently.

6 When tiny bubbles appear around the edge of the saucepan, carefully pour in the custard mixture. Using the wooden spoon, stir all the time until the custard thickens and boils. (If you do not stir it will become lumpy.)

7 Turn off the heat and stir for a few minutes longer. Move the saucepan away from the cooker and leave the custard until it is completely cold. You need to stir it occasionally to stop a skin forming on top.

8 When the custard is completely cold and the jelly is set, stir the yoghurt evenly into the custard. Take the glasses out of the refrigerator and pour custard on top of each jelly. Chill in the refrigerator.

9 Decorate each tilted jelly with chocolate buttons when you are ready to serve them.

Glossary

accompaniment something that is served with something else because they go well together e.g. cool yoghurt to accompany a spicy curry

allergic a person is said to be allergic to something if it causes them to have an unpleasant reaction – for example, some people are allergic to dairy products: if they eat them, they might get a rash on their skin or suffer a very bad headache

bacteria microscopic creatures which multiply quickly in warm conditions but are destroyed at high temperatures. Some are harmless but some can be poisonous

consumers people who buy products

dairy products food products made from milk – cheese, yoghurt, cream and butter

evaporation removing water by heating food

ferment change because of a chemical reaction in which gas is produced, e.g. a fruit yoghurt that has been kept too long may go fizzy or gassy

incubate to encourage the development of bacteria by keeping warm, e.g. during the making of yoghurt

internal organs delicate parts inside the body such as liver, kidney and heart

kilocalories traditional units used in the measurement of energy in our food e.g. 570 ml (one pint) of whole milk provides about 375 kilocalories

kilojoules modern units used in the measurement of energy in our food e.g. 570 ml (one pint) of whole milk provides about 1632 kilojoules (1 kilojoule = 4.2 kilocalories)

marinade a flavoured liquid in which food such as meat is soaked before being cooked, e.g. chicken may be left in a marinade made from natural yoghurt and spices before being cooked as a main meal

nutrients the chemical substances that make up food – protein, carbohydrate, fat, minerals and vitamins

nutritional value the type and quantity of nutrients in a food

pasteurization the heat treatment of milk to destroy bacteria

preservative something added to food to preserve it – this may be another food, e.g. sugar, or it may be a chemical preservative, e.g. ascorbic acid which is sometimes added to fruit yoghurts

preserve to treat a food so that it keeps for longer than it would naturally, e.g. UHT milk is preserved by being heated so that it lasts longer than fresh milk, if unopened

regurgitate bringing swallowed food back up into the mouth (something cows do naturally)

sour to go bad. When milk turns sour it is no longer fresh and it has an unpleasant taste and smell

soya milk 'milk' made from soya beans – popular with people who are allergic to animals' milk

sterilized treated to be made free from germs and harmful bacteria

Further reading

Developing Skills in Home Economics. C. Connell, D. Nutter, P. Tickner, J. Ridgwell. Heinemann Educational Australia, 1991

Food Around the World. Jenny Ridgwell and Judy Ridgway. Oxford University Press, 1986

Food from Dairy and Farmyard. Jacqueline Dineen. Young Library, 1984

Skills in Home Economics: Food. Jenny Ridgwell. Heinemann Educational, 1990

Index